Ashwater
DESK DIARY

2012

Ashwater
DESK DIARY

2012

ASHWATER
PRESS

Text is by Martin Plumb and photographs are by Ken Coton and from the Ashwater archive. Thanks are extended to Stephen Pound, David Lloyd and other Ashwater supporters. Acknowledgement is also due to Fulham worthies no longer with us: Alan Williams, Alec Stock, Peter Thomson and Reg Weller.

Special thanks are due to two Ashwater friends: Graham McDermott and Robert Fennell, the latter in particular for his invaluable help in the production of this publication.

Published in November 2011

The right of Ken Coton and Martin Plumb to be identified as the authors of this work has been asserted by them in accordance with the Copyright, Designs and Patent Act 1988.

Designed and published by
Ashwater Press
68 Tranmere Road, Whitton, Twickenham, Middlesex, TW2 7JB

www.ashwaterpress.co.uk.

Printed by Ian Allan Printing, Hersham, Surrey

ISBN 978-0-9562561-8-8

This first Ashwater diary appears at a great time for our club, celebrating ten years at the top, courtesy of our revered chairman, Mohamed Al Fayed. Ten years in the Premiership, Fulham's longest-ever spell at the highest level of English football – cheers!

The diary celebrates the rich history of our club, with photographs and illustrations encompassing over 100 years.

To all Ashwater supporters

Thank you for your many messages of support and encouragement. We hope you find this diary a worthy – and useful! – addition to our list of Fulham publications. Let's hope we're all together for another diary next year!

All comments and suggestions will be welcomed.

Front cover picture: Johnny Haynes leads out the Fulham team at the Cottage against West Ham in 1961.
Frontispiece: Gordon Davies in action at Walsall in 1982.
Above: fans in 1974.
Back cover picture: the Johnny Haynes statue outside the Craven Cottage ground.

FULHAM FOOTBALL CLUB

Founded 1879 – London's oldest professional league club.

SEASON 2011–2012

The Premiership

Arsenal – Emirates Stadium, N5 1BU – Tel: 020 7619 5003 – www.arsenal.com
Aston Villa – Villa Park, B6 6HE – Tel: 0121 327 2299 – www.avfc.co.uk
Blackburn Rovers – Ewood Park, BB2 4JF – Tel: 0871 702 1875 – www.rovers.co.uk
Bolton Wanderers – Reebok Stadium, BL6 6JW – Tel: 0844 871 2932 – www.bwfc.premiumtv.co.uk
Chelsea – Stamford Bridge, SW6 1HS – Tel: 0871 984 1955 – www.chelseafc.com
Everton – Goodison Park, L4 4EL – Tel: 0871 663 1878 – www.evertonfc.com
The Mighty Fulham – Craven Cottage, SW6 6HH – Tel: 0870 442 1222 – www.fulhamfc.com
Liverpool – Anfield, L4 0TH – Tel: 0151 263 2361 – www.liverpoolfc.tv
Manchester City – Etihad Stadium, M11 3FF – Tel: 0870 062 1894 – www.mcfc.co.uk
Manchester United – Old Trafford, M16 0RA – Tel: 0161 868 8000 – www.manutd.com
Newcastle United – St James' Park, NE1 4ST – Tel: 0844 372 1892 – www.nufc.co.uk
Norwich City – Carrow Rd, NR1 1JE – Tel: 01603 760 760 – www.canaries.co.uk
Queens Park Rangers – Loftus Road Stadium, W12 7PJ – Tel: 020 8743 0262 – www.qpr.co.uk
Stoke City – Britannia Stadium, ST4 4EG – Tel: 0871 663 2008 – www.stokecityfc.com
Sunderland – Stadium of Light, SR5 1SU – Tel: 0871 911 1200 – www.safc.com
Swansea City – Liberty Stadium, SA1 2FA – Tel: 01792 616 600 – www.swanseacity.net
Tottenham Hotspur – White Hart Lane, N17 0AP – Tel: 0844 499 5000 – www.tottenhamhotspur.com
West Bromwich Albion – The Hawthorns, B71 4LF – Tel: 0871 271 1100 – www.wba.co.uk
Wigan Athletic – DW Stadium, WN5 0UZ – Tel: 01942 774000 – www.wiganlatics.co.uk
Wolverhampton Wanderers – Molineux Stadium, WV1 4QR – Tel: 0871 222 2220 – www.wolves.co.uk

FOREWORD from
Stephen Pound MP

As any QPR supporter will tell you there are six reasons for hailing this 2012 Diary and nil against.

For me – and for most of my Fulham friends – the names of Coton and Plumb are guarantees of quality and this diary bears powerful witness to their skills.

Five decades in which we swung from the desperate to the delirious via the delighted and the despairing are captured by the pictures of the only other member of the Fulham family who can be called the Maestro.

It is great to see an Ashwater publication popping up again in 2011 and those of us whose Christmas present plans had been placed on hold can breathe again – although some of Ken's pictures will leave you breathless.

No-one else can show such a devotion to Fulham and football and no-one will ever again produce a pictorial history of our unique club that could come close to Ken's work.

It seems that as the chaos threatened to overwhelm us – especially during the 1980s – the still voices of calm and continuity came from Ken and Martin and there has never been a better combination than Coton and Plumb unless it is a bacon roll and brown sauce.

Martin Plumb is the poet of working class west London and describes the A4 corridor in a way that should be taught in every school. We've studied Shakespeare long enough – now is the time for Martin Plumb, and this diary provides evidence enough for the proposition.

To read Martin's description of some long ago titanic struggle and to then turn to Ken's photo, is to re-live that moment in a way that no modern technology can achieve. The fact that the end result was usually something nasty at the Baseball Ground or a camera challenging snowstorm at Wigan doesn't matter.

This is our history, the history of Fulham Football Club, recorded by two people who are so very much a part of that history.

Buy a copy each for friends and family – donate one to the Loftus Road trauma counselling centre but, above all, buy one for yourself. Carry it with you and whenever memory needs a spur, turn to these pages of perfect prose and pictures and be transported back to the Cottage.

This was the year in which we lost Roger Brown (turn to January 23). He will always be remembered in the memories of those who saw him by the greatest non-footballing football picture ever. Ken's shot of a sweat soaked and bloodied Roger Brown after the Lincoln game with a cigarillo in one hand and a mug of (allegedly) whisky in the other defines that great servant of the club – and proves how Ken not only watched the years unfold and our fortunes twist and turn but he was – and is – the recording angel to whom we turn as memory dims.

Treasure this book, this diary. It is, as Chris Coleman was wont to say, "class, sheer class".

Westminster, October 2011

2012

JANUARY
MON	.	2	9	16	23	30
TUE	.	3	10	17	24	31
WED	.	4	11	18	25	.
THU	.	5	12	19	26	.
FRI	.	6	13	20	27	.
SAT	.	7	14	21	28	.
SUN	1	8	15	22	29	.

FEBRUARY
MON	.	6	13	20	27	.
TUE	.	7	14	21	28	.
WED	1	8	15	22	29	.
THU	2	9	16	23	.	.
FRI	3	10	17	24	.	.
SAT	4	11	18	25	.	.
SUN	5	12	19	26	.	.

MARCH
MON	.	5	12	19	26	.
TUE	.	6	13	20	27	.
WED	.	7	14	21	28	.
THU	1	8	15	22	29	.
FRI	2	9	16	23	30	.
SAT	3	10	17	24	31	.
SUN	4	11	18	25	.	.

APRIL
MON	.	2	9	16	23	30
TUE	.	3	10	17	24	
WED	.	4	11	18	25	
THU	.	5	12	19	26	
FRI	.	6	13	20	27	
SAT	.	7	14	21	28	
SUN	1	8	15	22	29	

MAY
MON	.	7	14	21	28	.
TUE	1	8	15	22	29	.
WED	2	9	16	23	30	.
THU	3	10	17	24	31	.
FRI	4	11	18	25	.	.
SAT	5	12	19	26	.	.
SUN	6	13	20	27	.	.

JUNE
MON	.	4	11	18	25	.
TUE	.	5	12	19	26	.
WED	.	6	13	20	27	.
THU	.	7	14	21	28	.
FRI	1	8	15	22	29	.
SAT	2	9	16	23	30	.
SUN	3	10	17	24	.	.

JULY
MON	.	2	9	16	23	30
TUE	.	3	10	17	24	31
WED	.	4	11	18	25	.
THU	.	5	12	19	26	.
FRI	.	6	13	20	27	.
SAT	.	7	14	21	28	.
SUN	1	8	15	22	29	.

AUGUST
MON	.	6	13	20	27	.
TUE	.	7	14	21	28	.
WED	1	8	15	22	29	.
THU	2	9	16	23	30	.
FRI	3	10	17	24	31	.
SAT	4	11	18	25	.	.
SUN	5	12	19	26	.	.

SEPTEMBER
MON	.	3	10	17	24	.
TUE	.	4	11	18	25	.
WED	.	5	12	19	26	.
THU	.	6	13	20	27	.
FRI	.	7	14	21	28	.
SAT	1	8	15	22	29	.
SUN	2	9	16	23	30	.

OCTOBER
MON	1	8	15	22	29	.
TUE	2	9	16	23	30	.
WED	3	10	17	24	31	.
THU	4	11	18	25	.	.
FRI	5	12	19	26	.	.
SAT	6	13	20	27	.	.
SUN	7	14	21	28	.	.

NOVEMBER
MON	.	5	12	19	26	.
TUE	.	6	13	20	27	.
WED	.	7	14	21	28	.
THU	1	8	15	22	29	.
FRI	2	9	16	23	30	.
SAT	3	10	17	24	.	.
SUN	4	11	18	25	.	.

DECEMBER
MON	.	3	10	17	24	31
TUE	.	4	11	18	25	.
WED	.	5	12	19	26	.
THU	.	6	13	20	27	.
FRI	.	7	14	21	28	.
SAT	1	8	15	22	29	.
SUN	2	9	16	23	30	.

2013

JANUARY
MON	.	7	14	21	28	.
TUE	1	8	15	22	29	.
WED	2	9	16	23	30	.
THU	3	10	17	24	31	.
FRI	4	11	18	25	.	.
SAT	5	12	19	26	.	.
SUN	6	13	20	27	.	.

FEBRUARY
MON	.	4	11	18	25	.
TUE	.	5	12	19	26	.
WED	.	6	13	20	27	.
THU	.	7	14	21	28	.
FRI	1	8	15	22	.	.
SAT	2	9	16	23	.	.
SUN	3	10	17	24	.	.

MARCH
MON	.	4	11	18	25	.
TUE	.	5	12	19	26	.
WED	.	6	13	20	27	.
THU	.	7	14	21	28	.
FRI	1	8	15	22	29	.
SAT	2	9	16	23	30	.
SUN	3	10	17	24	31	.

APRIL
MON	1	8	15	22	29	.
TUE	2	9	16	23	30	.
WED	3	10	17	24	.	.
THU	4	11	18	25	.	.
FRI	5	12	19	26	.	.
SAT	6	13	20	27	.	.
SUN	7	14	2i	28	.	.

MAY
MON	.	6	13	20	27	.
TUE	.	7	14	21	28	.
WED	1	8	15	22	29	.
THU	2	9	16	23	30	.
FRI	3	10	17	24	31	.
SAT	4	11	18	25	.	.
SUN	5	12	19	26	.	.

JUNE
MON	.	3	10	17	24	.
TUE	.	4	11	18	25	.
WED	.	5	12	19	26	.
THU	.	6	13	20	27	.
FRI	.	7	14	21	28	.
SAT	1	8	15	22	29	.
SUN	2	9	16	23	30	.

JULY
MON	1	8	15	22	29	.
TUE	2	9	16	23	30	.
WED	3	10	17	24	31	.
THU	4	11	18	25	.	.
FRI	5	12	19	26	.	.
SAT	6	13	20	27	.	.
SUN	7	14	21	28	.	.

AUGUST
MON	.	5	12	19	26	.
TUE	.	6	13	20	27	.
WED	.	7	14	21	28	.
THU	1	8	15	22	29	.
FRI	2	9	16	23	30	.
SAT	3	10	17	24	31	.
SUN	4	11	18	25	.	.

SEPTEMBER
MON	.	2	9	16	23	30
TUE	.	3	10	17	24	.
WED	.	4	11	18	25	.
THU	.	5	12	19	26	.
FRI	.	6	13	20	27	.
SAT	.	7	14	21	28	.
SUN	1	8	15	22	29	.

OCTOBER
MON	.	7	14	21	28	.
TUE	1	8	15	22	29	.
WED	2	9	16	23	30	.
THU	3	10	17	24	31	.
FRI	4	11	18	25	.	.
SAT	5	12	19	26	.	.
SUN	6	13	20	27	.	.

NOVEMBER
MON	.	4	11	18	25	.
TUE	.	5	12	19	26	.
WED	.	6	13	20	27	.
THU	.	7	14	21	28	.
FRI	1	8	15	22	29	.
SAT	2	9	16	23	30	.
SUN	3	10	17	24	.	.

DECEMBER
MON	.	2	9	16	23	30
TUE	.	3	10	17	24	31
WED	.	4	11	18	25	.
THU	.	5	12	19	26	.
FRI	.	6	13	20	27	.
SAT	.	7	14	21	28	.
SUN	1	8	15	22	29	.

PERSONAL DETAILS

ADDRESSES

SERVIS

A B C D E F G H J
K L M N O P Q R S

When football was football: a neutral ground, a crowd of below 3,000 and the pitch markings just about visible through the snow and the frost. In an eerily empty stadium, Les Strong and Ronnie Goodlass launch another Fulham attack down the left wing. On a bitterly cold night in January 1981, a Gordon Davies goal sees Fulham win a third-round FA Cup second replay against Bury at the Hawthorns. Davies beats a young Neville Southall in the Shakers goal to get the result. After this marathon, Fulham predictably crashed out of the competition in the fourth round against Charlton at the Cottage just twelve days later.

DECEMBER 2011

Holiday

MONDAY
26

Holiday

TUESDAY
27

WEDNESDAY
28

THURSDAY
29

FRIDAY
30

SATURDAY
31

JANUARY 2012

SUNDAY
1

JANUARY 1963 – During the big winter freeze, with snow on the ground for several weeks, Fulham play no matches at all in January. The third-round FA Cup tie with West Ham is called off a record number of times and is finally resolved after a replay about seven weeks later.

It's life at the Putney End before the stand was built, and another rainy day spent dutifully following our team. Never mind the weather – and irrespective of the conditions and the situation – it's "Come on, you Whites!" as usual.

JANUARY 2012

MONDAY

2

TUESDAY

3

WEDNESDAY

4

THURSDAY

5

FRIDAY

6

SATURDAY

7

SUNDAY

8

JANUARY 1970 – Johnny Haynes plays the last of his 659 games for Fulham against lowly Stockport County at Craven Cottage. On a cold, grey afternoon a few diehard supporters witness a soulless encounter that ends 1–1. John Richardson scores Fulham's goal.

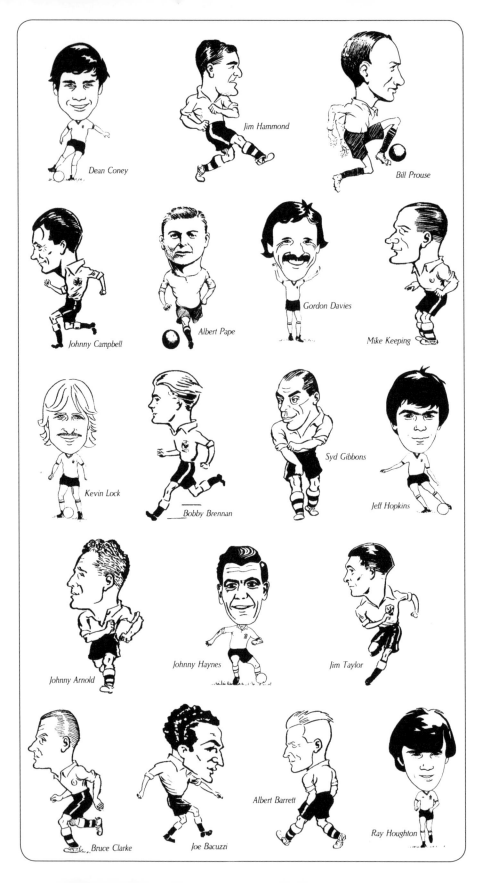

Dean Coney

Jim Hammond

Bill Prouse

Johnny Campbell

Albert Pape

Gordon Davies

Mike Keeping

Kevin Lock

Bobby Brennan

Syd Gibbons

Jeff Hopkins

Johnny Arnold

Johnny Haynes

Jim Taylor

Bruce Clarke

Joe Bacuzzi

Albert Barrett

Ray Houghton

MONDAY
9

TUESDAY
10

WEDNESDAY
11

THURSDAY
12

FRIDAY
13

SATURDAY
14

SUNDAY
15

JANUARY 1982 – Peter O'Sullivan played one season for Fulham and scores his only goal for the club in a 1–0 win against London rivals Brentford at Griffin Park.

Leaving the Cottage for an away trip in 1958 — with a gleaming coach and smart blazers and badges. In the coach are Tony Barton, Ken Collins (half hidden), Alan Mullery, Roy Bentley and Johnny Haynes; outside are Arthur Stevens, Trevor Chamberlain, Maurice Cook, Jimmy Hill, Jim Langley, Robin Lawler, Eddie Lowe, George Cohen, Frank Penn (trainer), and Bedford Jezzard (manager). Kneeling in front is Blueway's coach owner and driver Jimmy Andrews.

Watched by Don Rogers and Mel Blyth, Crystal Palace hardman Roy Barry makes a determined block to prevent Viv Busby from scoring in the Good Friday encounter at the Cottage in 1974. Barry Lloyd is close by monitoring developments. The Eagles won 3–1.

MONDAY

16

TUESDAY

17

WEDNESDAY

18

THURSDAY

19

FRIDAY

20

SATURDAY

21

SUNDAY

22

JANUARY 1992 – There is a perfect start to 1992 as Sean Farrell nets a hat trick at the Hawthorns in a memorable 3–2 win against West Bromwich Albion on New Year's Day.

Roger Brown – the Lionheart. One of the bravest both on the pitch and off it, taken from us far too soon. Roger appreciated what football had given him, being a 'late starter'. He is pictured here having just signed from Norwich City in 1980 for a significant £100,000. Although he played for the Whites for just four seasons, his centre-back pairing with 'Stroller' Gale was one of the best and most effective in Fulham's history.

MONDAY

23

TUESDAY

24

WEDNESDAY

25

THURSDAY

26

FRIDAY

27

SATURDAY

28

SUNDAY

29

 JANUARY 2002 – Lawrie Sanchez's Wycombe Wanderers give Premier League Fulham an almighty fright by holding them to a 2–2 draw at Adams Park in a third-round FA Cup tie, a late Steve Marlet goal saving Fulham's blushes. The Cottagers win a bruising replay 1–0.

Nice to see you again! Brazilian legend Pele is re-united with Alan Mullery less than three years after their epic encounter in the 1970 World Cup, where Brazil beat England 1–0. Pele's team Santos were in London for a friendly exhibition match at Craven Cottage in March 1973. Fulham won an entertaining game 2–1 with goals from Steve Earle and loan player Alan Pinkney. Pele naturally scored with a consolation textbook penalty, taking just one step forward for the kick. The Santos tour of England was clouded by their alleged late demands for 'additional payments' when the crowd were already in the stadium awaiting the start.

MONDAY
30

TUESDAY
31

FEBRUARY 2012

WEDNESDAY
1

THURSDAY
2

FRIDAY
3

SATURDAY
4

SUNDAY
5

 FEBRUARY 1964 – In just his second game, legend Steve Earle notches the first of his 108 Fulham goals against Blackpool in a 1–1 draw at Craven Cottage on leap year day. He later plays for Leicester City before emigrating to America.

A late Johnny Haynes goal has given Fulham a 2–2 draw at Bloomfield Road in 1965. An exhausted Bobby Keetch leaves the field pursued by a posse of young autograph hunters – and there's not a 'jobsworth' steward in sight! George Cohen and Bobby Robson discuss how Fulham have escaped with a point at Blackpool, as another young fan approaches the two England internationals.

MONDAY

6

TUESDAY

7

WEDNESDAY

8

THURSDAY

9

FRIDAY

10

SATURDAY

11

SUNDAY

12

 FEBRUARY 1972 – Goalkeeper Peter Mellor makes his Fulham debut at home to Bristol City. Fulham had won just one of their last ten matches in the Second Division, but Mellor's debut heralds a change of fortune. Fulham win the match 2–0, and eventually avoid relegation.

*Chairman Tommy Trinder (he of the famous chin) makes a presentation to Johnny Haynes'
mother, Rose. In the background are fellow director Noël 'Chappie' D'Amato and the
maestro himself. It's hard to guess what the present was. In the 1960s a typical
presentation would be of a cutlery set or a watch. It's possible that the picture shows
nothing more than a bunch of flowers in a less than elegant wrapping.*

MONDAY
13

TUESDAY
14

WEDNESDAY
15

THURSDAY
16

FRIDAY
17

SATURDAY
18

SUNDAY
19

FEBRUARY 1985 – A crowd of under 7,000 sees Kenny Achampong score the only goal of the game in an evening win over Oxford United. It is a fine solo effort on his debut. Oxford are promoted as champions at the end of the season.

A Fulham Football Club dinner at the Holborn Restaurant, London, March 18th 1907. This was just before the club's election to the Football League.

MONDAY
20

TUESDAY
21

WEDNESDAY
22

THURSDAY
23

FRIDAY
24

SATURDAY
25

SUNDAY
26

FEBRUARY 1991 – Phil Stant on his Fulham debut scores the only goal in the home victory over Preston North End in front of a crowd below 3,000. The former soldier plays just nineteen games for the club, but his five goals are crucial in helping Fulham avoid relegation.

*On an unseasonably warm October afternoon John Beck – all sweat and sideburns – patrols the
midfield at the Goldstone ground in 1978. Despite the best endeavours of the former QPR and Coventry
playmaker, Fulham lose this one with Brighton 0–3.*

MONDAY

27

TUESDAY

28

WEDNESDAY

29

MARCH 2012

THURSDAY

1

FRIDAY

2

SATURDAY

3

SUNDAY

4

 MARCH 1966 – Fulham win 5–2 at Villa Park during a run of five victories in the 'great escape' season. It's the first away league win for seventeen months. Earle and Leggat score twice, and Barrett gets one. The score equals Fulham's best-ever away victory in the top division.

Bobby Robson and George Graham watch closely as centre-forward Barry Bridges (not in picture) powers home a header for Chelsea's second goal at Craven Cottage in 1965, giving goalkeeper Tony Macedo no chance. The match didn't remain long in the memory as Fulham crashed to three first-half goals from the Pensioners. The only notable fact of the day was that Graham Leggat became Fulham's first-ever substitute, coming on for the injured Haynes.

MONDAY

5

TUESDAY

6

WEDNESDAY

7

THURSDAY

8

FRIDAY

9

SATURDAY

10

SUNDAY

11

MARCH 1974 – Following a 'sales pitch' from Alan Mullery, Bobby Moore signs for Fulham and makes his debut at home to Middlesbrough. In front of an 18,000 crowd it proves to be a tough game. Graeme Souness' team win 4–0 and are promoted as champions at the end of the season.

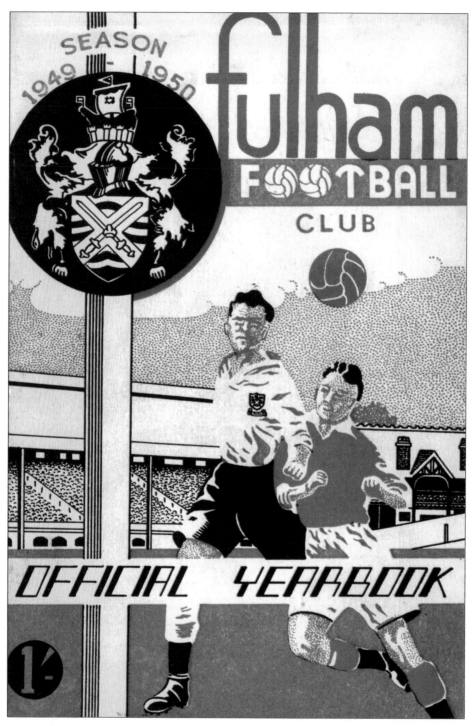

This was the cover of the club's handbook for 1949–50, Fulham's first-ever season in the top flight. In previous seasons, official programmes had been drab, black-and-white publications, but this yearbook presaged a notable change, as programmes for the new season in the First Division incorporated the colourful design shown here.

MONDAY

12

TUESDAY

13

WEDNESDAY

14

THURSDAY

15

FRIDAY

16

SATURDAY

17

SUNDAY

18

 MARCH 1987 – David Bulstrode is appointed Fulham chairman, and the club is threatened with merger with QPR, uprooting to Loftus Road, and a joint name of Fulham Park Rangers. A dispirited Fulham are thrashed 0–6 at home by Port Vale, the club's worst ever home league defeat.

A famous fan and a famous player pictured together in 2009. The fan, Peter Thomson, followed Fulham for over 50 years and wrote a series of books produced by Ashwater under the banner of 'Following The Fulham'. His untimely death in 2011 robbed supporters of further witty and erudite offerings from a much-loved headmaster on our favourite club. The player, Roy Bentley, was a stalwart for Fulham in the years 1956 to 1961. One of the club's genuinely great defenders, his associations with Chelsea, where he captained them to the league title in 1955, just go to show that not everything about the Stamford Bridge club is to be disdained.

MONDAY
19

TUESDAY
20

WEDNESDAY
21

THURSDAY
22

FRIDAY
23

SATURDAY
24

British Summer Time begins

SUNDAY
25

MARCH 1997 – Glenn Cockerill, in his only full Fulham season, scores his only Fulham goal in a 4–0 home victory over Scarborough. Debutant loan signing Christer Warren also scores his only Fulham goal. Fulham are promoted at the end of the season.

Long before Rory Delap, Ernest 'Jimmy' Langley was a master of the long throw; it was his trademark along with his crew-cut hair, bandy legs, overhead kicks and immaculately timed sliding tackles. Here he launches another missile into the Arsenal goalmouth in September 1963. A stickler for fair play, Langley was an England international full back who later, at the age of 38, took QPR to Wembley to lift the League Cup. He returned to Wembley with non-league Hillingdon Borough to play in the FA Challenge Trophy final at the age of 42, losing 2–3 to Telford United.

MONDAY

26

TUESDAY

27

WEDNESDAY

28

THURSDAY

29

FRIDAY

30

SATURDAY

31

APRIL 2012

SUNDAY

1

 MARCH 2007 – a limping Ian Pearce finds space to bobble a last-minute equaliser through the Portsmouth defence to give Fulham a 1–1 draw. It is a crucial point earned against relegation, but the team is showing little form, and Chris Coleman's tenure as manager is coming to a close.

Luis Boa Morte surges towards the penalty area during the third-round FA Cup tie at the Cottage in January 2001 against Manchester United and, oops, finds his foot hooked from under him as defender Wes Brown slides in with both feet off the ground. Nothing came of the incident. Fulham were a Division One (today's Championship) team at the time, but gave a good account of themselves, with Fabrice Fernandes scoring a fine first-half goal. However, a late goal by substitute Teddy Sheringham earned United a 2–1 victory.

APRIL 2012

MONDAY
2

TUESDAY
3

WEDNESDAY
4

THURSDAY
5

Good Friday holiday

FRIDAY
6

SATURDAY
7

SUNDAY
8

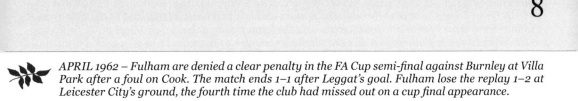

APRIL 1962 – Fulham are denied a clear penalty in the FA Cup semi-final against Burnley at Villa Park after a foul on Cook. The match ends 1–1 after Leggat's goal. Fulham lose the replay 1–2 at Leicester City's ground, the fourth time the club had missed out on a cup final appearance.

In 1981, manager Malcolm Macdonald is slowly re-moulding the Fulham side, and one of the young players he brings in, the combative Robert Wilson, is here making his presence felt in midfield up at Carlisle. Dean Coney has come through the juniors and has just been introduced to the side as well. Fulham were clear of any relegation fears and the team finally achieved promotion the following season. Unfortunately Fulham lost this particular encounter at Brunton Park 2–3 with a final goal in a Fulham shirt from centre back Geoff Banton making a rare start.

APRIL 2012

Easter Monday holiday

MONDAY
9

TUESDAY
10

WEDNESDAY
11

THURSDAY
12

FRIDAY
13

SATURDAY
14

SUNDAY
15

APRIL 1974 – Bobby Moore scores his only Fulham goal on Good Friday at home to Crystal Palace. Unfortunately, Palace were already three goals ahead, and won 3–1. In true Fulhamish fashion, Fulham win the return four days later 2–0 with goals from Viv Busby and Les Barrett.

Two pictures from the match at the Cottage against Crystal Palace in October 2000.
Above: The visitors know all about the threat that Luis Boa Morte possesses as four hard-pressed
Selhurst players try to prevent the flying winger getting in a telling cross or shot.
Below: Lee Clark fires home one of his two goals that evening.
Louis Saha gets the other goal in the 3–1 victory, and Fulham maintain their perfect start to the season
– eleven games and eleven wins. The team are seemingly unstoppable, scoring at a rate of almost three
goals a game. The next three games – draws with Wolves and Sheffield Wednesday and a defeat by
Preston – slightly derail the Fulham juggernaut, but the Whites are soon back in the groove. They lose
just four more times in the league all season and cruise to the championship with 90 league goals and
101 points.

MONDAY
16

TUESDAY
17

WEDNESDAY
18

THURSDAY
19

FRIDAY
20

SATURDAY
21

SUNDAY
22

APRIL 1986 – Fulham play nine games in twenty-eight days in April at the tail end of the season. They win just two of their last nineteen games and finish bottom of the table, nine points adrift of the next club, Middlesbrough.

Two headers from different eras. Above: Joe Gilroy gets in a header in Fulham's 3–0 victory at Coventry in November 1967; this may have been the goal Joe scored that afternoon (our photographer cannot remember...). Below: Simon Morgan scores one of his two (yes, two!) goals in the 4–0 victory over Burnley in December 1998 on the way to the Division Two championship under Kevin Keegan.

St George's Day
– patron saint of
England

MONDAY
23

TUESDAY
24

WEDNESDAY
25

THURSDAY
26

FRIDAY
27

SATURDAY
28

SUNDAY
29

 APRIL 1994 – Substitute Rob Howarth scores the winning goal in a 2–1 victory over Brentford at Griffin Park; it proves to be his only league goal. However, just one victory in the final five games of the season sees Fulham fall into the basement division for the first time ever.

Six defenders can't stop him and Ivor Davies nets Fulham's first goal against Sheffield United in a Boxing Day morning kick-off. It's only December but the pitch is already well worn. Fulham win this encounter with the Blades 2–1, the other goal being a Kevin Lock penalty. Note chairman Ernie Clay's publicising of his Huddersfield company on the advertising hoarding at the side of the ground. In the Blades squad were World Cup star Martin Peters (then 37) and ex-Fulham veteran John Ryan. There were two other playing connections – full back John Cutbush was in the Sheffield squad together with a very young Gary Brazil. United were managed by Harry Haslam who had spent time at the Cottage as a scout and an assistant to Bobby Robson in 1968–69.

In the Wembley dressing-room after Fulham's only appearance in the FA Cup final,
which was lost 0–2 to West Ham, there is tangible dejection, as well as discarded
shinpads, plastic cups and blacked out boots.
By the time you come to write in this diary in May 2012, Fulham may be appearing in
their second FA Cup final – well, we can hope and we can dream!

MONDAY

30

MAY 2012

TUESDAY

1

WEDNESDAY

2

THURSDAY

3

FRIDAY

4

SATURDAY

5

SUNDAY

6

MAY 1967 – Bobby Robson plays the final game of his career – an uneventful 2–3 home defeat by Nottingham Forest. Sir Bobby played 370 games for Fulham in two spells, scoring 80 goals. He left to manage Vancouver in Canada before returning as Fulham manager a few months later.

Promotion from Division Three was achieved in 1971 under manager Bill Dodgin, Jnr. Victory in the last match of the season – at home to Preston – would have brought Fulham the championship, but the match was lost 0–1, and Fulham had to settle for runners-up spot. The manager refuses to celebrate with the team on the Cottage balcony after the Preston defeat, but players Fred Callaghan, Reg Matthewson, Jimmy Dunne, Les Barrett and Vic Halom are delighted to take a bow.
A few days later the team celebrates with wives and girlfriends at a dinner at a London hotel.

Early May bank holiday

MONDAY
7

TUESDAY
8

WEDNESDAY
9

THURSDAY
10

FRIDAY
11

SATURDAY
12

SUNDAY
13

MAY 1977 – Needing a point to ensure safety in Division Two, goal-shy Fulham go mad and crush Orient 6–1, actually being 6–0 up at half-time. John Mitchell bags a career-best four goals. The match is notable for being Bobby Moore's final appearance at Craven Cottage before retirement.

FULHAM
FOOTBALL CLUB
OFFICIAL HANDBOOK
SEASON 1968·9
PRICE 2/-

WHERE TO PARK

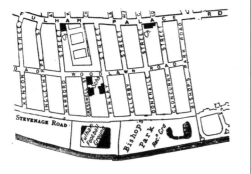

PARKING

with the exception of Fulham Palace Road, Finlay Street and
Stevenage Road, all streets shown on map are available for
parking during the match.

TICKETS FOR AWAY MATCHES
Club Address and Advance Booking Information

Aston Villa — Villa Park, Trinity Road, Birmingham, 6.
12/6d. and 10/- (available two weeks in advance).

Birmingham City — St. Andrews Ground, Birmingham, 9.
10/- (available two weeks in advance).

Blackburn R. — Ewood Park, Blackburn, Lancs.
10/- (available two weeks in advance).

Blackpool — Bloomfield Road, Blackpool, Lancs.
11/-, 9/-, 8/6d. available in advance.

Bolton Wanderers — Burnden Park, Bolton, Lancs.
10/6d., 9/6d. (available four weeks in advance.)

Bristol City — Ashton Gate, Bristol, 3.
Prices: 12/6 each (available two weeks in advance)

Bury — Gigg Lane, Bury, Lancs.
10/6d. (available two weeks in advance).
7/6d., 8/6d. and 9/- seats available on day only).

Cardiff City — Ninian Park, Cardiff, Glam.
12/6d., 7/6d. (available two weeks in advance).

Carlisle Utd. — Brunton Park, Carlisle, Cumb.
9/- (available 10 days in advance).

Charlton Ath. — The Valley, Floyd Road, London, S.E.7.
10/- (available four weeks in advance).

Crystal Palace — Selhurst Park, London, S.E.25.
10/-, 7/6d. (available in advance).

Derby County — Baseball Ground, Derby.
12/-, 10/-, 9/- (available on the day only).

Huddersfield T. — Leeds Road Ground, Huddersfield, Yorks.
10/6d. (Available 10 days in advance).

Hull City — Boothferry Park, Hull, Yorks.
12/6, 12/-, 8/6d. (available 7 days in advance)

Middlesbrough — Ayresome Park, Middlesbrough, Yorks.
10/6d., 8/6d. (available two weeks in advance).

Millwall — The Den, Coldblow Lane, London, S.E.14.
9/- (available 7 days in advance).

Norwich City — Carrow Road, Norwich, NOR 22.T.
10/-, 9/-, 8/- (available two weeks in advance)

Oxford Utd. — Manor Road Ground, Beech Road, Headington, Oxford.
10/-, 8/- (available two weeks in advance).

Portsmouth — Fratton Park, Portsmouth, Hants.
12/-, 10/- (available 10 days in advance).
Also 10/- and 7/6d. available on the day only.

Preston N. E. — Deepdale, Preston, Lancs.
9/6d., 8/6d. (available two weeks in advance).

Sheffield Utd. — Bramall Lane, Sheffield, S2 4SU, Yorks.
13/6d., 11/-, 9/-, 7/6d. (available two weeks in advance)

MONDAY
14

TUESDAY
15

WEDNESDAY
16

THURSDAY
17

FRIDAY
18

SATURDAY
19

SUNDAY
20

 MAY 1982 – Due to the weather and consequent fixture congestion, Fulham play six league games in eighteen days in this month in their attempt to climb out of Division Three. The epic 1–1 draw with Lincoln City and Roger Brown's header ensure a happy ending for the tired Cottagers.

Kevin Lock (Mr Reliable) scores from the penalty spot to put Fulham into the lead in the match against Huddersfield Town at the Cottage in February 1982. The electronic scoreboard helps identify the moment. The match was eventually drawn 2–2, and was the club's fourth draw out of five league matches that month. The team began winning again in March and achieved promotion at the end of the season.

MONDAY
21

TUESDAY
22

WEDNESDAY
23

THURSDAY
24

FRIDAY
25

SATURDAY
26

SUNDAY
27

MAY 1995 – Nick Cusack rounds off a mediocre Fulham season with a hat trick in a 5–0 demolition of Rochdale at Craven Cottage. It is the biggest win of the season for Ian Branfoot's men. Gary Brazil and Martin Thomas net the other goals.

Brian Greenaway latches on to a headed forward pass from Chris Guthrie and slots the ball past the Stoke goalkeeper, despite the attentions of Geoff Scott. This was in just the second minute of the match in October 1978. Tony Gale netted a fine second to seal Fulham's win. Fulham were in great form and the 2–0 win came despite Stoke counting Howard Kendall, Mike Doyle and Garth Crooks in their side. It also wasn't a happy return for striker Viv Busby who came on early as a Stoke substitute.

MAY 2012

MONDAY
28

TUESDAY
29

WEDNESDAY
30

THURSDAY
31

JUNE 2012

FRIDAY
1

SATURDAY
2

SUNDAY
3

 JUNE 1965 – With funds raised from a number of sources, chairman Tommy Trinder finally sees work begin on the construction of the first Hammersmith End stand at Fulham at a cost of around £25,000. Although a pretty rudimentary structure, it served its purpose for many years.

A speedy George Best shows a clean pair of heels to Orient defender Peter Allen in the final home match of the 1976–77 season. Fulham scored six without reply in the first half but eased off in the second, actually 'losing' the second half 0–1. It was the first time Fulham had scored more than five goals at home in a league game for over fourteen years.

JUNE 2012

Spring bank holiday

MONDAY

4

The Queen's Diamond Jubilee holiday

TUESDAY

5

WEDNESDAY

6

THURSDAY

7

FRIDAY

8

SATURDAY

9

SUNDAY

10

JUNE 1972 – An angry Tommy Trinder disbands the affiliated Fulham Supporters Club after criticism from fans over the sacking of Bill Dodgin just one season after promotion. Supporters were critical that Dodgin had not been given enough time or money to rebuild his small squad.

Lee Clark shows impeccable close control as he evades a Forest defender during the match at the Cottage in February 2001. Fulham won the match with a goal from Louis Saha, on the way to amassing 101 points for the Division One season and clinching the championship with a margin of ten points over second-placed Blackburn Rovers.

MONDAY

11

TUESDAY

12

WEDNESDAY

13

THURSDAY

14

FRIDAY

15

SATURDAY

16

SUNDAY

17

JUNE 1984 – Ray Harford is confirmed as Fulham manager after the shock departure of Malcolm Macdonald. The team that so narrowly missed promotion is being slowly dismantled; Roger Brown leaves mid-season, and Tony Gale and Sean O'Driscoll exit the club in the close season.

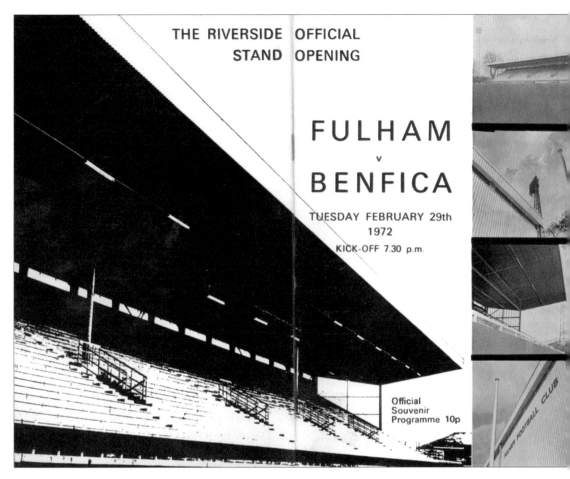

THE RIVERSIDE OFFICIAL
STAND OPENING

FULHAM
v
BENFICA

TUESDAY FEBRUARY 29th
1972
KICK-OFF 7.30 p.m.

Official
Souvenir
Programme 10p

This is the back and front of the club's programme for the match against Benfica that celebrated the opening of the Riverside stand in 1972.

The colour pictures on the cover (which were taken by Ashwater's own Ken Coton) are rather poor reproductions, partly because they were the first attempt by the printers to produce in-house the plates needed to print them. Four separate printing plates are required to print a colour picture and the process of producing what are called the separations is highly specialised – though nowadays it is done entirely by computer. In 1972 it was just becoming possible for small operators to produce their own separations (which were made on film), but it still needed considerable skill. The Fulham printers at the time, TW Pegg & Sons, used the Benfica programme as a try-out of their new technology.

The new stand was opened about three months late due to problems with the weather, and with supplies and costs. In many respects the stand is basically unaltered since its completion almost forty years ago. Fulham took the match quite seriously and were two goals to the good inside the first fifteen minutes thanks to a strike from Steve Earle and a glancing header from Roger Cross. Benfica pulled a goal back just before half-time. Cross scored his second with the aid of a deflection to restore Fulham's two-goal advantage and even a late thunderbolt from World Cup star Eusebio couldn't deny Fulham a 3–2 win.

MONDAY
18

TUESDAY
19

WEDNESDAY
20

THURSDAY
21

FRIDAY
22

SATURDAY
23

SUNDAY
24

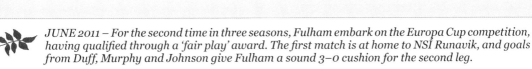

JUNE 2011 – For the second time in three seasons, Fulham embark on the Europa Cup competition, having qualified through a 'fair play' award. The first match is at home to NSI Runavik, and goals from Duff, Murphy and Johnson give Fulham a sound 3–0 cushion for the second leg.

Although Jimmy Conway scored two goals at home to Cardiff in August 1974, he picks up a booking that afternoon. Here he gets ticked off by referee Alex Lees, whilst Cardiff's Alan Impey walks away and Fulham's Barry Lloyd nervously adjusts his socks.

Viv Busby scored Fulham's two other goals in the 4–0 victory, and the match is famous for his brilliant solo goal when he sped down the left wing, taking out five defenders, before slotting the ball past the Cardiff goalkeeper. It is rated by many as one of the finest post-war goals scored at the Cottage.

Fulham scored nine goals in the season's opening four matches but eventually ended the season in mid-table. But the club did get through to the FA Cup final at Wembley.

MONDAY

25

TUESDAY

26

WEDNESDAY

27

THURSDAY

28

FRIDAY

29

SATURDAY

30

JULY 2012

SUNDAY

1

 JULY 1966 – Fulham have a player in the team that lifts the World Cup for England at Wembley. A proud George Cohen lines up at number two alongside Everton's Ramon (Ray) Wilson, described by Sir Alf Ramsey as 'the best pair of full backs England ever had'.

Long before the arrival of squad numbers, the players here all seem to have a separate training kit number. It seems that as usual Fulham can't even afford the requisite number of corner flags. However, posing happily for the camera in December 1972 are 'The Three Musketeers' who played a vital role in Fulham's fortunes between 1969 and 1974 – Jimmy Conway the speeding winger on the right wing, Steve Earle the darting centre forward in the middle and Les Barrett the flying flanker down the left. In the days of soccer loyalty, between them they made over 1,000 appearances for Fulham and netted just short of 275 goals – wow! Jimmy Conway had missed the first half of the season after sustaining a nasty injury on the opening day and had just returned to the side.

MONDAY

2

TUESDAY

3

WEDNESDAY

4

THURSDAY

5

FRIDAY

6

SATURDAY

7

SUNDAY

8

 JULY 1971 – The bulldozers are in and Fulham begin building a stand on the riverside terrace of the ground, to be known as the 'Eric Miller Stand'. Fulham's state of the art half-time electronic scoreboard which stood atop the tea bar was re-housed within the Hammersmith End stand.

Peter Marinello was dubbed the 'Scottish George Best' after some storming displays for Hibernian as a youngster. This encouraged Arsenal to pay, for the first time, a six-figure sum (£100,000) to buy him. It was a gamble which early on looked like a sound investment especially after a debut goal against Manchester United. However, the bright lights and associated lifestyle coupled with homesickness appeared to lead him astray and he failed to fulfil his early promise. Within three years he was with Second Division Portsmouth. He continued his nomadic lifestyle with spells in Scotland, Australia and America. He arrived at Fulham in the summer of 1979 at almost 30. He showed early promise with a goal in the Anglo-Scottish Cup and the winner (his only league goal) against Preston North End; however, he was sent off in the next home match. He played just twenty-seven games for the Whites and finished his career in Scotland after leaving Craven Cottage at the end of one season.

MONDAY
9

TUESDAY
10

WEDNESDAY
11

THURSDAY
12

FRIDAY
13

SATURDAY
14

SUNDAY
15

JULY 1989 – The controversial but much-loved former chairman of Fulham, Tommy Trinder, dies aged eighty. A life-long fan and dedicated chairman for seventeen years, he used Fulham in his repertoire as a comedian to keep Fulham in the public eye, employing benign humour.

In July 1972, Alec Stock is appointed Fulham's new manager, and here a press photographer gets down to the business of snapping him at the Cottage. Stock wastes no time in re-building the team following the sacking of his former QPR colleague Bill Dodgin. He signs full back John Cutbush (right) on a free transfer from Tottenham and then raids the club again to secure the return of Alan Mullery for a fee around £60,000; Mullery had spent eight years away. He then breaks Fulham's transfer record again, by buying the titanic centre-half Paul Went (left) from Charlton Athletic for a fee of £80,000. He is also responsible for giving Les Strong his chance early that season, initially on the right wing but later as a full back.

MONDAY
16

TUESDAY
17

WEDNESDAY
18

THURSDAY
19

FRIDAY
20

SATURDAY
21

SUNDAY
22

JULY 1998 – Following the club's failure in the play-offs, Kevin Keegan takes sole charge of the team for his first full season. In a dazzling display of attacking football, Fulham soar to the championship of the old Division Two, finishing fourteen points clear of second-placed Walsall.

Fulham players take part in a charity darts tournament at the Lord Palmerston pub in the Kings Road in 1962. Throwing a dart is manager Bedford Jezzard, whilst behind him Bobby Robson looks on. Also looking intently at the board are Jim Langley and Maurice Cook in the foreground of the picture. The two players distracted from the action are George Cohen and Eddie Lowe. Would it be possible for such an event to take place with today's Fulham stars? It's difficult to envisage without agents, minders and entourage, but Ashwater happily challenges the current first team to a game of arrows...

MONDAY
23

TUESDAY
24

WEDNESDAY
25

THURSDAY
26

FRIDAY
27

SATURDAY
28

SUNDAY
29

 JULY 2001 – Fulham announce that they have agreed terms for the transfer of goalkeeper Edwin Van der Sar from Juventus, the fee a reported £7 million. It is a statement of intent from the promoted club with regard to their future ambitions.

In the early days of 'sponsorship', the late Fulham coach Bill Taylor, nicely attired, takes pleasure in posing with three lovely ladies from Swan National, a car rental company with whom Fulham had an association in the Seventies. It was probably the equivalent of today's 'strategic partnerships' or 'corporate alliances' or 'marketing opportunities' or ... well, you get the idea.

MONDAY

30

TUESDAY

31

AUGUST 2012

WEDNESDAY

1

THURSDAY

2

FRIDAY

3

SATURDAY

4

SUNDAY

5

 *AUGUST 1960 – In their first midweek away match of the season Fulham crash 2–7 at St James'
Park, being 1–5 down to Newcastle United at half time. Fulham are torn apart by a side that
concedes over one hundred league goals in the season and is relegated.*

In Manchester United's only recent season outside the top flight, Barry Lloyd's cross eludes everyone during their visit to the Cottage in October 1974. Defender Jim Holton and goalkeeper Alex Stepney are in a muddle in the middle whilst Scottish defenders Martin Buchan and Stewart Houston look on. Also in the picture is Brian Greenhoff. Jimmy Conway tries to catch the ball and Alan Mullery and Bobby Moore add weight to the attack. Fulham took the eventual champions all the way and were unlucky to lose 1–2 in the televised match. United won thanks to two goals from their ace marksman Stuart Pearson. Viv Busby's goal five minutes from the end came too late to influence the result.

MONDAY

6

TUESDAY

7

WEDNESDAY

8

THURSDAY

9

FRIDAY

10

SATURDAY

11

SUNDAY

12

 AUGUST 1972 – Alec Stock sees the task in front of him as Fulham are well beaten 0–3 on the opening day of the season at Hillsborough. To add to the misery Stan Horne is sent off and Jimmy Conway sustains a bad injury that rules him out for more than three months.

July 1971, and building work is well underway on the new riverside stand. Already demolished is half of the riverside terracing, but the flagpoles remain.

In dark (actually red) socks, Jimmy Conway surveys the scene on a cold and murky January afternoon in 1973. The sandy, rutted pitch is in poor condition, a far cry from today's bowling green surfaces. Jim scored the second goal that day in a 2–1 victory against Middlesbrough, the first coming from an Alan Mullery penalty. The furrows of sand were said to be an attempt to improve the draining properties of the pitch, though they may have been the coach's ideas of getting the point over on how to use the 'channels'.

MONDAY
13

TUESDAY
14

WEDNESDAY
15

THURSDAY
16

FRIDAY
17

SATURDAY
18

SUNDAY
19

 AUGUST 1981 – Despite a very early Gordon Davies goal, Fulham slump to a 1–2 home defeat against neighbours Brentford on the first day of the season. The Brentford team contains ex-Fulham Paul Shrubb, future Fulham Terry Hurlock and former Chelsea hardman Ron Harris.

For some reason this crowd at Ayresome Park don't appear to be too impressed and a couple shout abuse. However, Stan Brown with clenched fists cares not a jot, Fulham have just scored and are on their way to a rare away win against Middlesbrough. The 2–1 victory in August 1973 comes courtesy of goals from Roger Cross and Les Barrett. Stan Brown was known as the 'players' player', loyal, reliable and versatile. He played in just short of 400 Fulham games in his twelve years at the club and featured in every outfield position (numbered 2 to 11 in those days) for the team. He was rightly awarded a testimonial against Chelsea during the 70–71 season.

MONDAY
20

TUESDAY
21

WEDNESDAY
22

THURSDAY
23

FRIDAY
24

SATURDAY
25

SUNDAY
26

 AUGUST 1995 – Two goals each from Michael Mison and Martin Thomas give Fulham the ideal start to the season with a 4–2 victory over Mansfield Town. However, by February the Whites had slumped to their lowest ever league position, but recovered under new manager Micky Adams.

It looks more like a day for ice creams and buckets and spades than for football. However, on a boiling afternoon in August 1973 Bill Taylor and Alec Stock (seated) oversee a pre-season friendly with Fulham pitted against Newport County in Wales. For the record, a full-strength Fulham side lost 1–2 that day, with Steve Earle netting Fulham's goal, but bounced back to beat Norwich City in a friendly a couple of days later.

Summer bank holiday

MONDAY

27

TUESDAY

28

WEDNESDAY

29

THURSDAY

30

FRIDAY

31

SEPTEMBER 2012

SATURDAY

1

SUNDAY

2

SEPTEMBER 1964 – Dave Metchick nets a hat trick for Fulham in their 3–1 evening home win over Birmingham City. This gives him six goals in his opening four games, scoring in each. Despite this excellent start he is transferred to Leyton Orient less than three months later.

A famous squad photographed in 1958 that went on to win promotion to the top flight for only the second time in Fulham's history.
Standing: Eddie Lowe, George Cohen, Roy Bentley, Tony Macedo, Joe Stapleton, Jim Langley; seated: Graham Leggat, Jimmy Hill, Maurice Cook, Johnny Haynes, Trevor Chamberlain.

MONDAY

3

TUESDAY

4

WEDNESDAY

5

THURSDAY

6

FRIDAY

7

SATURDAY

8

SUNDAY

9

SEPTEMBER 1970 – On a warm evening, Fulham put previously unbeaten Bradford City to the sword with an emphatic 5–0 win at Craven Cottage. The forwards were numbered 7 to 11 in those days and each of the five scored that night. Fulham were promoted at the end of the season.

Fulham's FA Cup run in 1974 lasted just three matches including a replay against Leicester City. The first match was a 1–0 victory at home to Preston North End, which was witnessed by under 7,000 people on a gloomy January afternoon. Here the teams are trudging back on to the pitch for the second half, and heading past the wheelchair are John Mitchell, Preston's Nobby Stiles, and John Lacy. The ex-World Cup winner Stiles is looking as if he would rather be somewhere else. It wasn't a great day for Norbert as he was booked later in the match and eventually substituted.
Fulham's winner that day came from John Conway, the younger brother of Jimmy. John was a talented and committed player who was very unlucky with injuries during his time at Craven Cottage. The match marked the first full appearance in the senior side of Scottish youngster John Dowie who had a commendable game.

MONDAY
10

TUESDAY
11

WEDNESDAY
12

THURSDAY
13

FRIDAY
14

SATURDAY
15

SUNDAY
16

SEPTEMBER 1982 – Goalkeeper Gerry Peyton is badly injured early on in the game at Middles-brough. This was long before the days of substitute goalkeepers, and defender Kevin Lock takes over in goal and Paul Parker comes on. A talented Fulham team cruises to a resounding 4–1 win.

Another Sunday at Cold Blow Lane and Strongy finds himself making a rare appearance upfield at Millwall. Never the happiest of hunting grounds for Fulham – even when the team are doing well and promotion looks assured – the old Millwall ground proves to be yet another banana skin. The free-scoring Fulham attack puts away three goals that day, but the usually resolute defence goes missing and concedes four as the Cottagers are edged out 3–4 in this match in April 1982. Despite this reverse, Fulham squeeze into a promotion slot against Lincoln on the final evening of the season three weeks later.

MONDAY

17

TUESDAY

18

WEDNESDAY

19

THURSDAY

20

FRIDAY

21

SATURDAY

22

SUNDAY

23

 SEPTEMBER 1996 – Richard 'Chippy' Carpenter scores on his debut at Darlington. In a very tough encounter feelings run high and the Fulham side gives as good as it gets. The Whites win 2–0, the other goal coming from Paul Watson. It is Fulham's seventh victory in the opening nine games.

A delighted Rodney Marsh watches Maurice Cook's cross-shot enter the Leeds net at the Cottage in March 1965. Billy Bremner looks displeased and Norman Hunter is grounded. The goal against the Yorkshire high-fliers gives Fulham a 2–1 lead but a late Bobby Collins goal ensures a 2–2 draw. This picture was taken a few months before the erection of the first Hammersmith End stand and cranes can be seen in the wood mill behind.

The entertaining but unpredictable Marsh was top scorer for Fulham that season in the First Division (today's Premiership) with seventeen league goals. A year later Fulham predictably sold him to Third Division Queen's Park Rangers.

MONDAY
24

TUESDAY
25

WEDNESDAY
26

THURSDAY
27

FRIDAY
28

SATURDAY
29

SUNDAY
30

SEPTEMBER 2006 – Late goals from Brian McBride and Carlos Bocanegra give Fulham a 2–1 win at St James' Park after Newcastle had taken the lead early in the second half. Jimmy Bullard is badly injured in a tackle with Scott Parker and does not play again that season.

From one defender to another – George Cohen presents a player of the year award to a young Jeff Hopkins, who had made his debut on the final day of the 1980–81 season. Hopkins established himself as a mainstay of the Fulham defence both as a full back and centre back for the next six years. The tall defender made over 250 appearances for Fulham. He had his fair share of injuries and at one stage his playing days seemed over, but he went on to have a career that finally encompassed over 500 games. He became a Welsh international winning sixteen caps, fourteen whilst at Craven Cottage.

MONDAY

1

TUESDAY

2

WEDNESDAY

3

THURSDAY

4

FRIDAY

5

SATURDAY

6

SUNDAY

7

OCTOBER 1967 – Fulham sign Joe Gilroy from Clyde for a significant fee of £20,000. He plays well, contributing seven goals in his first two months before injury halts his progress. He ends the season with a very respectable ten goals despite Fulham's relegation.

In March 2001, Barry Hayles turns and fires home an early first-half goal against Bolton Wanderers after a lot of Fulham pressure. However the team failed to add to the goal and the Trotters netted an equaliser. Despite significant pressure, a rugged and resolute Bolton defence held firm and left the Cottage with a 1–1 draw. A late-season surge saw the Lancashire side promoted back to the top division in third place behind Fulham and Blackburn Rovers.

To balance things out for that season, below is a picture from a rare off-night during that eventful period; it shows Lee Clark crowded out by some determined Preston resistance. After a record eleven consecutive wins at the start of the season, it proved to be unlucky thirteen for Fulham, and North End escaped with a 0–1 victory that was probably just about deserved on the October evening. In that promotion season, Fulham lost just one other league match at Craven Cottage.

MONDAY
8

TUESDAY
9

WEDNESDAY
10

THURSDAY
11

FRIDAY
12

SATURDAY
13

SUNDAY
14

OCTOBER 1972 – Les Strong scores his first goal for Fulham in a 2–0 win over Blackpool at Craven Cottage. He manages to get another four goals over the next ten years and was for many years Fulham's top scorer in Europe with two goals in the Anglo-Italian tournament in 1973.

Is this David Hamilton presenting Alec Stock with a Manager of the Month award, or is it Alec presenting our David with an award for the most challenging haircut of 1975? Answers on a postcard, please.

MONDAY
15

TUESDAY
16

WEDNESDAY
17

THURSDAY
18

FRIDAY
19

SATURDAY
20

SUNDAY
21

OCTOBER 1982 – Macdonald's Fulham stun high-fliers Newcastle at St James' Park. In a televised match, the Whites put on a breathtaking show, winning 4–1 with a superb all-round passing game and clinical finishing. Ray Houghton's long-range shot is a candidate for goal of the season.

The caption could read 'Chin and gin', though it's probably red wine in the glass. Fulham have boasted two famous chins in recent history – that of former chairman Tommy Trinder, and this one belonging to a true football great, Jimmy Hill. Here, proudly sporting a Fulham tie with an instantly recognisable Fulham crest, Jim is toasting a success on the road to securing Fulham's future in the 1990s.

Jimmy Hill – player, manager, TV groundbreaker, pundit, soothsayer, visionary – and saviour! Without his intervention in 1987, plus the unending support in time and money from a number of dedicated Fulham supporters, there would be no Fulham Football Club today with all the glitter (and the jobs and departments) that comes with it. The industrious Hill was signed from Brentford in 1952 as a half back and also played as an inside forward. He played almost 300 games for Fulham and scored over 50 goals. He was also, during his playing career, the chairman of the PFA and the players' representative at Fulham, helping to abolish the maximum wage. After retiring with a knee injury, he took over as manager of Coventry City, revived an ailing club and took them to the First Division (Premiership) in a manner similar to our recent ascent. He soon turned his attention to television, and helped pioneer Sunday afternoon TV football with 'The Big Match' alongside co-presenter Brian Moore. He became one the game's first pundits discussing the technical side of football and pointing out the rights and (more often) the wrongs. He pioneered the three points for a win principle. He was outspoken, often controversial and at odds with the FA and also his fellow pundits, but was always highly respected.

Cheers, Jim!

MONDAY
22

TUESDAY
23

WEDNESDAY
24

THURSDAY
25

FRIDAY
26

SATURDAY
27

British Summer Time ends

SUNDAY
28

OCTOBER 1994 – Striker Mark Stallard joins Fulham on a month's loan from Derby County. He plays four games, fails to scores in the first three, but nets a hat trick in his final game to bring off a 4–0 win over Exeter City at Craven Cottage, with Simon Morgan getting the other goal.

Goalkeeper Gary Bailey saves comfortably from the on-rushing Gordon Davies and the situation looks pretty routine in the fourth-round FA Cup match against Manchester United in January 1979. However, the incident sparks an all too familiar Premiership style 'handbags' mêlée. Centre half Gordon McQueen and Sammy McIlroy seem to be the 'agent provocateurs' for United, whilst Terry Bullivant and Chris Guthrie slug it out for Fulham, keeping Ivor out of the action. Experienced referee Ken Styles wades in as peacemaker, and in those days, a strong word was all that was necessary. For the record, Jimmy Greenhoff gave First Division United the lead in the first half, but John Margerrison gave Second Division Fulham a deserved equaliser with a marvellous headed goal in the second half. In the replay, an unlucky Fulham side were edged out 0–1. (How often have we heard that in the FA Cup at Old Trafford?) United went to the final at Wembley that year where they were beaten 2–3 by Arsenal in one of the best ever finals with three goals in the last ten minutes.

OCTOBER 2012

MONDAY

29

TUESDAY

30

WEDNESDAY

31

NOVEMBER 2012

THURSDAY

1

FRIDAY

2

SATURDAY

3

SUNDAY

4

 NOVEMBER 1968 – Bobby Robson is sacked by Fulham after just ten months in charge at Craven Cottage. Johnny Haynes reluctantly takes over as player manager and in his first game, despite looking shaky in defence, Fulham pull off a fine 4–3 victory over Huddersfield Town the Cottage.

Season 1976/77

All winners and queries will be dealt with at the Pools Office. Goals are timed by a qualified Official F.A. Referee and his decision is final.

All claims must be made within 7 days from the day of the match. Registered under Betting, Gaming and Lotteries Act 1963.

BUY AN EXTRA TICKET and increase your chances of winning an exciting prize. YOU COULD GO HOME £50 BETTER OFF . . .

Kenmar Press (Printers) Ltd. Sidney Road · N22 4LS · 01-888 7221

FULHAM FOOTBALL CLUB IMPROVEMENT SOCIETY
Craven Cottage, S.W.6
Promoter: M. SMITH

LEAGUE MATCH   5p
FULHAM v SHEFF UTD

GOLDEN GOALS

£50
to be paid on the time of 1st goal

£10
to be paid on the time of 2nd goal

Consolation prize of £1 for one second either side of the winning goal times or a long playing EMI RECORD. If the score is 0-0 the ticket marked "No Score" wins £60. If the score is 1-0 the winning time wins £60.

This is Your Goal Time:
MINS.   SECS.

N⁰   **11 44**

Goal Times will be announced over the public address system during and after the match. They will also be available from the Pools Office after the match

YOUR NUMBER IS:

N⁰   **4682**

Listen out at half-time for your number and you may have won of three exciting prizes.

PRIZE ONE
Ten Gallons of Jet Petrol kindly donated by CONOCO L

PRIZE TWO
Case Horlimann Sternbrau Lag donated by the Managing Director HORLIMAN (UK) LTD. MR. KEN PLATTS

PRIZE THREE
Hamper of Groceries (Value £6 kindly donated by A & O EUROPE'S FAVOURITE GROCER

NO OTHER PRIZE GIVEN IN LIEU

The golden goal tickets were one shilling (5p) in the mid-seventies. To win you needed to have the exact minute and second of the goal as relayed over the PA at Fulham (in this case 11 minutes 44 seconds). Only one ticket had 'no score' on it, meaning that a maximum of 5,401 tickets could be sold. The first prize seems pretty mediocre – ten gallons of petrol; presumably you didn't have to collect it after the match. Even by today's standards (£60) it's hardly an inspiring prize. The golden goal tickets complemented a fund-raising scheme for supporters (agents) who were sent pink tickets every week to sell to family and friends. A bit like today's scratchcards, these cards contained a number of 'games'. Some of the prizes were quite good, though the most often won prizes were pairs of tights! Not too much use for the male winners (except at weekends maybe!). The promotion was run for many years at Fulham by the genial Johnny Hartburn from an office in the Stevenage Road stand. John was an ex-player of some repute, having played over 300 games on the wing and scoring almost 100 goals in a career that encompassed QPR, Watford, Millwall and Leyton Orient. He died in 2001 aged 80. Below: a flutter ticket twenty years later was still modestly priced at £1.

FULHAM FLUTTER

01-11-97 Match V. CHESTERFIELD   TKT NO. 2140

FULHAM F.C. DEVELOPMENT ASSOCIATION
CRAVEN COTTAGE, STEVENAGE ROAD, LONDON SW6 6HH
Promoter: N. Smith

TICKET COST £1.00.

50% OF GROSS TAKE PAID IN PRIZES AFTER THE DEDUCTION OF EXPENSES
DRAWN AT HALF TIME

All proceeds go directly to help your club

All monies after the deduction of prizes and expenses shall be deemed a donation to the aims of the promoting Society
Full list of previous winners available from Promoter at the above address. Not to be sold to persons under 16 years.

MONDAY

5

TUESDAY

6

WEDNESDAY

7

THURSDAY

8

FRIDAY

9

SATURDAY

10

SUNDAY

11

NOVEMBER 1974 – After superb displays against holders Wolverhampton Wanderers and West Ham, Second Division Fulham are knocked out of the League Cup 0–3 by another First Division side, Newcastle United, at St James' Park. Malcolm Macdonald scores one of United's goals.

The hand of fate is in evidence as Barry Hayles (second left) nets Fulham's opening goal past Brad Friedel in the match against Blackburn Rovers in the initial season back in the top flight (February 2002). A physical encounter ended with a 2–0 victory for the home side. Purist Jean Tigana was, not for the first time, critical about the over-physical nature of some teams in the Premiership. It was a good job that Fulham won this match as from this point the team struggled and picked up just two draws from the next nine games, pushing them to the brink of an unthinkable relegation. However an excellent win at eventual fifth-placed Leeds United, thanks to a Steed Malbranque goal, helped turn the tide and Fulham survived.

MONDAY
12

TUESDAY
13

WEDNESDAY
14

THURSDAY
15

FRIDAY
16

SATURDAY
17

SUNDAY
18

NOVEMBER 1983 – Second Division Fulham play three epic encounters with League champions Liverpool in the third round of the League Cup. Kevin Lock's penalty gives Fulham a 1–1 draw at home, and Lock repeats the feat at Anfield. Liverpool win the second replay (at Fulham) 1–0.

It's 7th May 1977, and this is Bobby Moore's last appearance at the Cottage before hanging up his boots. He played one more match for Fulham, away at Blackburn, the last match of the season. This home match was against Orient and before the game Moore was given a hero's accolade. Here he is interviewed for television, but note that the camera (with its Mickey Mouse ears) is not a video camera, but a film camera. This was well before the age of electronics. The film had to be processed and edited before its pictures could be seen and transmitted. (The ears contained the roll of film as it passed through the camera.)

MONDAY
19

TUESDAY
20

WEDNESDAY
21

THURSDAY
22

FRIDAY
23

SATURDAY
24

SUNDAY
25

NOVEMBER 1993 – Fulham lose a crazy match down in Exeter by a score of 4–6, a result made worse by the fact that Exeter did the double over Fulham and were still relegated. It was the first time ten goals had been scored in a Fulham league match for almost thirty years.

Steed Malbranque scores the first goal in Fulham's 2–1 victory over Dinamo Zagreb in the UEFA Cup competition in October 2002. The match was played at Queens Park Rangers' ground during Fulham's two-year absence from Craven Cottage. Against very decent opposition, Fulham went through comfortably with a 5–1 aggregate score. Sadly the Cottagers were edged out in the next (third) round, losing 1–2 on aggregate to Hertha Berlin; they were frustrated by a goalless 'home' draw having lost 1–2 away in the first leg, courtesy of a bizarre own goal from 'the Lone Ranger' Facundo Sava.

Tony Gale made his debut at just seventeen in 1977 and immediately looked a player of great class with control, timing, an eye for a pass and an excellent reading of the game. Although primarily a centre back, Gale could play just as capably in midfield and at one stage early in his career scored six goals in just twelve league games.

After a very promising start to 1977–78, Fulham looked capable of a return to the First Division, but sadly fell away after February, and just two wins in the final seventeen league games meant that the Cottagers finished in a mediocre mid-table position.

Here 'Stroller' comes away with the ball in March 1978 during the Easter Bank Holiday fixture against Mansfield Town. Despite his best efforts, it was an uninspiring Fulham performance and they went down 0–2. Tony Gale played for nearly 20 years in a career that took in almost 600 games; he is now a respected pundit on television. Many consider it a scandal that Gale won nothing more than a solitary England U-21 cap. He should have played for England, and if his career had been with Man United and Liverpool rather than Fulham and West Ham maybe he would have done so.

MONDAY

26

TUESDAY

27

WEDNESDAY

28

THURSDAY

29

FRIDAY

30

DECEMBER 2012

SATURDAY

1

SUNDAY

2

 DECEMBER 1961 – Fulham lose all five league matches in December and fail even to register a goal. By the end of February they had lost eleven league matches in a row, their worst ever run of consecutive defeats. From March they recovered just enough to avoid relegation – by one point.

Phone
Renown
5 6 2 1

Telegrams
Fulhamish
Walgreen

FULHAM
FOOTBALL CLUB
(Fulham Football & Athletic Company, Ltd.)

CRAVEN COTTAGE
FULHAM, S.W.6

FIXTURES
1957-58

Our Playing Staff

John Haynes (Captain)
English International.
Roy Bentley
English International.
Ian Black
Scottish International.
Tony Barton
James Bowie
William Clarkson
George Cohen
John Chenhall
Trevor Chamberlain
Kenneth Craggs
Kenneth Collins
John Doherty
Roy Dwight
Harry Durso
David Edwards
Kenneth Hewkins
(South Africa).
James Hill
England B. International.
Bedford Jezzard
English International.
John Key
Peter Kavanagh
Derek Lampe
Ernest J. Langley
England B. International.
Robin Lawler
Irish International.
Edward Lowe
English International.
Roy Lambden
Gerald Morgan
Elliott Macedo

Brian O'Connell
Maurice Pratt
Arthur Stevens
Joseph Stapleton
Harry Taylor
Trevor Watson
Alfred Wilson
James Weir

AMATEURS

John Bond
Lawrence Brown
Michael Cloherty
Michael Cross
London County Youth.
Roy Dobson
Middlesex County Youth.
Terence Evans
Anthony Haynes
Desmond Kempson
John Martin
Peter Mathews
Allen Mullery
London Schoolboys.
Ian Rankin
Terence Smart
Richard Smith
Robert Shields
Edward Speight
Brian Sullivan
English Schoolboy
International.
Peter Wollaston
London Schoolboys.

ADMISSION CHARGES

Admission to

Ground	-	2/- (Boys 1/-)
Enclosure	- -	- 3/-
Stands	4/-, 5/-, 6/-, 7/6 & 8/6	

COMBINATION MATCHES
Admission to all parts 1/-

Join the SUPPORTERS' CLUB

applications to :—

Fulham F.C. Supporters' Club

Gen. Sec., **A. Skinner**
Golden Lion,
Fulham High Street,
S.W.6

or at Huts on ground.

The Players', Directors and
Management, extend a Welcome
to Craven Cottage,
to all our Supporters.

Chas. B. Dean
Chairman

It is interesting to note that apart from Allen (sic) Mullery and a cameo from Brian Sullivan, none of the amateurs made the grade. Even more surprising perhaps is that eight of the professional playing staff mentioned failed to make even one appearance in the first team.

MONDAY

3

TUESDAY

4

WEDNESDAY

5

THURSDAY

6

FRIDAY

7

SATURDAY

8

SUNDAY

9

DECEMBER 1976 – Fulham's game against Oldham survives frost and freezing weather and television crews turn up to see Fulham put on a great show, crushing the visitors 5–0. John Mitchell and Teddy Maybank each score twice and the mercurial George Best also nets a beauty.

So often discussed, so often revered and so rarely seen. Two goals down to Tottenham Hotspur at half-time at Loftus Road in September 2002, Fulham turn the tables completely with three goals in the final third of the game. Junichi Inamoto halves the deficit and Steed Malbranque levels from the spot after the referee's assistant spots a penalty area foul on Barry Hayles. Then right at the death Sylvain Legwinski curls home a delightful winner just inside a post. The Spurs players are stunned whilst the Fulham players are 'over the moon'. Legwinski, just by the penalty spot, turns away in celebration to embark on the obligatory run of delight. A memorable 3–2 win.

MONDAY
10

TUESDAY
11

WEDNESDAY
12

THURSDAY
13

FRIDAY
14

SATURDAY
15

SUNDAY
16

 DECEMBER 1981 – Macdonald's improving side from the Third Division play a fourth-round League Cup tie at White Hart Lane. Fulham exit the competition to Spurs 0–1 thanks to a Micky Hazard goal. Tottenham are outplayed for long periods and look relieved to win the match.

A Third Division squad picture taken at the start of the 1969–70 season, which followed two consecutive relegations. Under manager Bill Dodgin the team achieved a respectable fourth position at the end of the season, and gained promotion at the end of the next campaign.
Back row: Wilf Tranter, Reg Matthewson, Vic Halom, Brian Williamson, Ian Seymour, Dave Roberts, John Gilchrist, Danny O'Leary; middle row: Steve Earle, Johnny Haynes, Stan Brown, Stan Horne, Jimmy Conway, Cliff Jones, Frank Large; front: Barry Lloyd, Mike Pentecost, Les Barrett, Fred Callaghan, Dave Moreline.

MONDAY
17

TUESDAY
18

WEDNESDAY
19

THURSDAY
20

FRIDAY
21

SATURDAY
22

SUNDAY
23

 DECEMBER 1992 – The Cottagers sign John McGlashan on a month's loan from Millwall. He plays five games for Fulham and even manages a goal from midfield that earns a point in a 1–1 home draw with Blackpool just before Christmas in front of a crowd of below 4,000.

...and 'Happy Christmas' greetings from Ashwater!
The 1978 Christmas card was a replica of the front cover of the official programme for that season. The lower card was the club's offering for 1972. It was printed on dimpled paper and the photograph was not very sharp. The helicopter belonged to businessman and Fulham director Eric Miller. Manager Alec Stock is standing second left; others in the photo are directors (from left) Guy Libby, Charles Dean, Tommy Trinder and Noël 'Chappie' D'Amato.

MONDAY
24

Christmas Day holiday

TUESDAY
25

Boxing Day holiday

WEDNESDAY
26

THURSDAY
27

FRIDAY
28

SATURDAY
29

SUNDAY
30

DECEMBER 2004 – A long-range screamer from Papa Bouba Diop in the dying moments gives Fulham a 1–1 Monday night draw against eventual champions Manchester United at Craven Cottage. Diop celebrates his goal with a run virtually all round the pitch.

Rory Hamill prepares to confront the Scunthorpe keeper during Fulham's home match on 30th January 1996. The occasion is often quoted as attracting Fulham's lowest-ever home league attendance, with just 2,176 hardy souls turning up to witness the 1–3 defeat.

The 'Don't Kill Fulham' hoarding in the background just underlines the club's precarious position at the time, as there was a serious threat of the club going out of existence with the ground turned over to luxury housing.

P.S. Both Fulham books of statistics by Fulham's historian give the attendance for the match at home to Carlisle in April 1986 as just 2,134. So, the hunt for the lowest attendance requires Holmes and Watson. The match programme following the 1986 Carlisle encounter (Hull City) has the Carlisle attendance as 4,951, probably unlikely as it is exactly the same figure as for the Crystal Palace match about three weeks earlier. The programme after the Hull one is Charlton Athletic. Fulham were so hard up those days that they used the original programme from the postponed match in February, hence the Carlisle match had not then been played. The final home programme of the season against Huddersfield Town gives the attendance as 2,134 and if accurate is indeed the lowest league attendance. It is the only formal reference to that attendance.

DECEMBER 2012

MONDAY
31

JANUARY 2013

New Year's Day holiday

TUESDAY
1

WEDNESDAY
2

THURSDAY
3

FRIDAY
4

SATURDAY
5

SUNDAY
6

 JANUARY 1965 – In a third-round FA Cup home tie against then Fourth Division Millwall, First Division Fulham take a 3–0 lead but Millwall fight back to claim an unlikely 3–3 draw. In the white-hot atmosphere at the Den for the replay, Fulham are beaten 0–2 with embarrassing ease.

227

FULHAM FOOTBALL CLUB LIMITED
CRAVEN COTTAGE · STEVENAGE ROAD · LONDON SW6

Fulham Football Club
1st Team Match
Date and Kick-off to be announced
in the National Press.

Price £1.00

BLOCK	RIVERSIDE STAND	
	HAMMERSMITH END (Turnstiles 34 & 35)	
TU	ROW	SEAT
	G	**17**

FULHAM 1st TEAM MATCH

RIVERSIDE STAND

£1.00

BLOCK **TU**

ROW **G**

SEAT **17**

THIS IS NOT A TICKET

Ticket Office: Craven Cottage Stevenage Road London SW6 6HH   CONCESSION   ADULT

dabs.com   BARCLAYS

TO BE RETAINED   fulhamfc.com   TO BE GIVEN UP   TO BE GIVEN UP

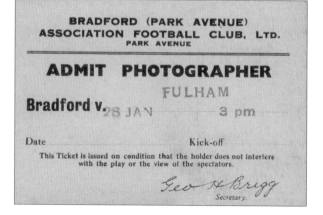

BRADFORD (PARK AVENUE)
ASSOCIATION FOOTBALL CLUB, LTD.
PARK AVENUE

ADMIT PHOTOGRAPHER

FULHAM

Bradford v. 28 JAN   3 pm

Date _____   Kick-off _____

This Ticket is issued on condition that the holder does not interfere
with the play or the view of the spectators.

Geo. H. Brigg
Secretary.

Keep taking the TOOFIF! And check out the TOOFIF website.
And don't forget this website:

Books on Fulham Football Club published by Ashwater Press:

FULHAM'S GOLDEN YEARS
FULHAM – THE TEAM 1903–1995
FULHAM'S GOING UP!
THE COTTAGERS' JOURNALS
FOLLOWING THE FULHAM
FULHAM PHOTOS
PANDORA'S FULHAMISH BOX
FOLLOWING THE FULHAM INTO EUROPE
FOLLOWING THE FULHAM AROUND THE GROUNDS
A FULHAMISH COMING OF AGE
TALES FROM THE RIVERBANK – SEASONS 1965–66 AND 1966–67
TALES FROM THE RIVERBANK – SEASONS 1967–68 AND 1968–69
JOHNNY HAYNES – THE MAESTRO
FOLLOWING THE FULHAM – THE PREMIERSHIP YEARS
THE MICKY ADAMS PROMOTION SEASON – 1996–97
WHEN FULHAM WENT TO WEMBLEY
FOLLOWING THE FULHAM ON A EUROPEAN TOUR

For availability of these books please see www.ashwaterpress.co.uk or contact Ashwater Press.

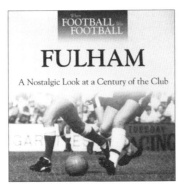

You might like to look out this book from publishers Haynes which has been put together
from the Mirror archives by Fulham fan Richard Allen. It's available on Amazon.

The way we were...

ASHWATER
PRESS